Jason Pegler
Mentoring

The 3 Laws And 21 Ways To Mental Health Empowerment

Jason Pegler

chipmunkapublishing
the mental health publisher

Published by
Chipmunkapublishing
United Kingdom

http://www.chipmunkapublishing.com

Copyright © 2015 Jason Pegler

ISBN 978-1-78382-176-1

Chipmunkapublishing gratefully acknowledge the support of Arts Council England.

Introduction

I've written this book to give people with mental illness additional tools to improve their lives. As with anything in life how successful they are depends on how much action they take and what attitude they use whilst taking this action. They also need to take action that is relevant to consistently improving their mental wellbeing. If you want to be well then study how to be well.

I have been working with people with mental illness since the year 2000. Above everything else the ones that get better are the ones that have the right attitude. In order to achieve happiness and independence one needs to take 100% responsibility for the situation one is in in one's life. Too many people with mental illness fail to see this truth and end up in a negative cycle of unnecessary pain.

My goal in this book/program is to give you the personal development, coaching and mentoring tools to dramatically transform your life; to take you to the next level of happiness and abundance no matter where you are at. Although, I am very passionate about personal development and mentoring as my life has been greatly enhanced by them, I have big concerns about the mentoring industry and its 'gurus'. Often, clients are manipulated and brainwashed into thinking they need the next more advanced course, seminar or revolutionary approach or they will be missing out on so much inside that they will only be half of a person or empty in some way, shape or form.

This program is designed to inspire you and show you how to live the life of your dreams now. It makes you responsible for your own life and gives you some amazing techniques to reprogram your mind and life for you to be a happier you and a more useful person in society.

Have faith, be strong, vigilant, enjoy the ride and most of all focus on being happy now. In order to benefit from Mental Health Mentoring you need to enjoy the journey along the way and not just the destination. The secret is that the destination is always evolving and so are you. Your mental health is either declining or improving every day. It never sits still so please join me and choose to improve it.

Jason Pegler

3 Laws:

Mental Health Mentoring

21 Ways – the first letter of each word, and the final way is to sign a contract with yourself at the end of the book to commit to following through.

You can mentor yourself if you learn to coach yourself. They are one and the same.

Mental

M Mindset

E Empowerment

N NLP– Pseudo Science/placebo or best brain tool ever

T Transformation (i.e. the way you think. Look react. Be positive, take action)

A Attitude

L Longevity (consistency in all these attitudes)

Health

H Heart (get your heart right)

E Exercise

A Admit (admit where you really are in your health)

L Love

T Truth

H Hypnosis (self-hypnosis – where you focus is where you end up)

Coaching

C Congruency (everything in your life needs to be congruent)

O Organised

A Action

C Coach yourself

H Highlight

I Inspiration

N Nurturing (every single day)

G Goal Setting daily it's a must

Mental - M

Mindset

Getting your mindset correct is essential.

Where you focus is where you end up.

Our mind controls our thoughts, thoughts create our actions, actions determine where we end up.

Whatever we tell ourselves in our mind on a momentary basis determines our outlook, moods, happiness, mental health and whether we perceive ourselves as successful or not.

Mental - E

Empowerment

Empowerment is such an important tool in your own life to maximize your own mental health and is a real blue print in mental health mentoring. Empowerment is an overused and misunderstood term.

To empower yourself you have to realise that it's a constant process that can never be finite. Empowerment is an ongoing action, attitude, motivation and outcome.

At every moment in our lives we have two different voices in our heads. One that says we can do it and one that says that we cannot. We may be able to move into the now by accident or on purpose if we look through a window for example where we live in the present and forget the past and future momentarily. This dream like state or day dream like state is very powerful but what people with mental illness need is the ability to stop the negative voices inside their head and flip them around into the positive. You know when you have a great idea to do something and then you tell yourself immediately I will do that now and then as soon as you have said that to yourself your other half says I'll do it later... Well that is you becoming a victim of the law of diminishing intent...

People who experience mental illness often lack the confidence to do things. One part of them says I can do that and then the other part of themselves say I can't. Just stop for a moment and think of someone you really admire... Someone who has created something unique... For example Steve Jobs from Apple, Bill Gates who founded Microsoft, Usain Bolt the record breaking sprinter; all of these people had a vision, believed and acted on that vision before it actually happened.

In fact, anyone who has been successful at anything has taken action on something where if they had listened to the negative voice that was inside their head they would have achieved far less. Empowerment is a constant battle and struggle against your negative self – you have to pump yourself up. A great metaphor for this is physical exercise. Think of weight lifting and body building in particular. The more you work on your muscles and the more pain you go through the more defined your muscles become.

Arnold Schwarzenegger used to train in the gym 5 hours a day. He said that he would push himself even more on the parts of his body where he deemed himself the weakest. Also, someone once asked Mohammed Ali how many press ups he did a day. He said that he only counts the ones that hurt. Both Arnold and Mohammed have amazing empowerment strategies built into their psyches.

Some people just give up, it's as simple as that and they are the ones that disempower themselves and self-manifest their mental illness. I want you to keep moving along, keep pushing, and make the positive voice on your head louder and the negative voice softer. Keep telling yourself that you can do something in the moment as many times as you can. This is something that you will need to do hundreds, maybe even thousands of times a day – tell yourself to do it now and keep telling yourself to do it now. Then, just start doing it.

The people who make the most mistakes are also often the most successful. The ones who are prepared to keep trying something many times and in different ways are the ones that come to the top of the tree in any industry. The same is true for whatever subject you are concerned with business, family, relationships, fitness, love...

Empowerment and Mental Health Empowerment is all about saying yes to life and saying yes to yourself; accepting what has happened to you, taking responsibility for it and then reprogramming your mind so that you work out a strategy and implement it. Take yourself to the next level and live the life of your dreams now... and now... and now... that's it...

hundreds of times a day... thousands of times a day. Stop procrastinating and get on with it. And enjoy the ride.

Mental - N

NLP– Pseudo Science/placebo or best brain tool ever

Neuro-linguistic programming (NLP) is an approach to communication, personal development, and psychotherapy created by Richard Bandler and John Grinder in California, United States in the 1970s. Its creators claim a connection between the neurological processes ("neuro"), language ("linguistic") and behavioral patterns learned through experience ("programming") and that these can be changed to achieve specific goals in life.

The views on NLP range from a pseudo-science that is at best a placebo to the greatest mind technique ever invented.

I first got into NLP or something similar when watching the Paul McKenna TV show in the early nineties. I got really into personal development when I read Anthony Robbins' Unlimited Power in the year 2000. To his credit Anthony Robbins has his own unique system that is probably even more famous than NLP itself. His book and seminars helped me turn my life around and raise my standards constantly. Whenever I have any self-doubt I go back to Anthony Robbins as I believe he is unparalleled in the personal development industry.

I have trained Practitioner and Master Practitioner Level with Richard Bandler. Bandler is an amazing teacher and I highly recommend him as well. Everyone leaves his Seminars wiser and happier. Interestingly, Richard says himself that 70% of what people learn and take with them at the seminars is absorbed on an unconscious level and only 30% is on a conscious level.

We all have different senses, sight, hearing, feelings, taste and smell (in NLP they call them visual, auditory, kinaesthetic, gustatory, and olfactory). How we use these senses determines how we experience our lives. So, the more we are aware of each of these senses the more we can alter them in our favour to design the states and the lives that we want.

NLP is focused on modelling excellence and eliciting the strategies of successful people and copying them. This resonates with mentoring. A great example would be a golf coach: if you want to be good at golf then learn from a golf coach or go even further and learn from one of the greats. Watch interviews with Tiger Woods, Jack Nicklaus. Gary Player, Arnold Palmer, Phil Mickelson, etc. See how they think, watch how they play, study every aspect of their stroke and how they go about their games.

People with mental illness really do fill their minds with junk. Get rid of the junk by replacing the negative images you visualize and replace them with positive ones: make the negative voices positive, make the nasty smell nice. Of all the NLP exercises John La Valle, who is Bandler's main business partner and co trainer with his wife Kathleen, told me in October 2013 that the timelines work the best so here one for you.

Believe me this will save you a lot of time reading NLP and not understanding any of it. If you just want the positive effect, I recommend Paul McKenna's "I Can Make You Happy" and "Instant Confidence" above anything else. They are both really powerful and effective programs and the CD comes free with the paperback on Amazon. Play at night for the most positive effect.

Mental - T

Transformation (i.e. the way you think. Look react. Be positive, take action)

In order to live your life to the fullest and to mentor yourself to be mentally well, you have to transform the way you think, behave, and act.

A great way to mental health mentor yourself to do this is to break down every aspect of your life into different sections and ask yourself the following question: "In what 3 ways am I going to raise my standards and get better at this aspect of my life?"

"In what 3 ways am I going to raise my standards and get better at this aspect of my life?"

Physical Fitness

1.

2.

3.

No matter what level you are at you can always improve. If you are obese and do not work out, start walking 1 mile a day, take the stairs instead of the elevator, or do 5 sit ups. If you are an Ironman pro push your watt threshold another 2 watts... That can make a massive difference over a 180km bike leg and could be the difference between being and not being on the Ironman podium.

Love

1.
2.
3.

If you are happily in love with your partner already then that's great but you can still improve the relationship. Instead of giving a kiss when you get home from work, kiss for a moment longer or give as hug as well or look your partner in the eye while you kiss them. Say you love your partner more often or show you love them by doing something to help out without having to be asked. If you do not have a partner then work on loving yourself more and see how that makes you feel.

Managing my Money

1.
2.
3.

If you already manage your money then that's great but you can always improve. Increase the amount of money you save per month by 1%. Work out more precisely what your incoming or outgoings are.

> *"Create a vision of who you want to be and then live into that picture as if it were already true."* - Arnold Schwarzenegger

Being inspired by a s makes you realise that: you can make up who you want to be. This is the ultimate self-motivation for anyone. So use it.

Spirituality

1.
2.
3.

Parenting

1.
2.
3.

Friendships/Socialising/Peer group

1.
2.
3.

Every challenge we face improves our skills – break free from comfort zones.

Managing my time

1.
2.
3.

Managing My Confidence

1.
2.
3.

Mental - A

Attitude

Take complete possession of your own mind, you can only control your own mental attitude.

You will find when you are ready to seek.

Mental - L

Longevity

Keep working on living the life of your dreams moment by moment, minute by minute, hour by hour, day by day, week by week, month by month, year by now and before you know it when you stop and reflect where you were, you will be amazed at how far you have come.

Just keep doing little by little, day by day. Start projects and start your to do list. The slower you start them the quicker you will finish with them as you are doing them.

The effect of the action you take will be compounded over time.

Great paintings and people are created slowly – piece by piece.

Health

H Heart (get your heart right)
E Exercise
A Admit (admit where you really are in your health
L Love
T Truth
H Hypnosis (self-hypnosis – where you focus is where you end up)

Health - H

Heart

In order to be the best mental health mentor for yourself you must ask yourself what your heart really wants and allow yourself to feel.

Feeling your heart applies to being at one with yourself and in your relationships. Let yourself go. Feel that frisson, that's right, feel that tingling sensation in every aspect of your body.

If you have an inkling to do something that you know is the right thing to do, then do it. It's not just your conscience that will feel good, your heart will shine through.

Feel the right thing to do, and then just do it. This applies to every aspect of your life. Whether it is when you are looking for love, whether you are in a relationship, with your parents, family, and friends – only you know what feels right for you. Nobody else.

No matter what you say to other people whether they are friends, counsellors, coaches or psychiatrists, they just mirror your attitude towards your own feelings. It is you and you alone that has decide what to do with your heart. Be true to yourself and you will lead a life of fulfilment and happiness.

Health - E

Exercise

The more you exercise the happier you will be. It's good to exercise early in the day if you can as then you benefit from the endorphin rush and knowing you have exercised for the rest of the day. Exercise what you believe is right for you but don't be a lightweight or a cop out. There are so many different types of sports and exercises that you can do that it should not matter if you have an injury or are overweight. People who do not exercise lack one thing to exercise and that's not time. People who exercise frequently are just as busy as people who don't. They are just more motivated to exercise than people who don't exercise enough.

Think of your health today and in the future. Know that every time you exercise you are doing something that benefits your health today and tomorrow. At the time of writing this I have been exercising between six and fifteen hours a week for twenty months. I've completed one Ironman race (that's a 2.4 mile swim, a 112 mile bike ride and a 26.2 mile run all in a row on the same day) and a dozen shorter races during this period. I'm now training for my second Ironman race where I intend to go three hours quicker than the first time. I have found that by exercising so much I have been more successful in other areas of my life. This includes finances, relationships and happiness.

It is no secret that exercising is not only good for your body and health but it also for your happiness and other aspects of your life, as well. Being physically fit makes you more decisive, gives you more confidence in other areas of your life, more energy and get up and go to experience more in life yourself and with those you love.

Health - A

Admit where you really are in your health

Here are some exercises to help you decipher how your health really is.

Your health is inclusive of different aspects of your life and condition. How you look, what you eat, how you feel, etc. All of these different things are relevant to how 'healthy' and therefore how happy you are.

Look at yourself naked in a full-length mirror and be honest about your body shape. Is it what you really want? If not, then take a photo of yourself and keep it somewhere and vow to go back to it every month for the next 12 months. Write the date down in your calendar on your phone.

This may sound drastic and it is. However, it will get you in the emotional state to really admit what your body really looks like, then imagine how you want it to be. Think of an athlete or a famous person whose type of body you would like and put that on your vision board or on your fridge. This way you will see that body every time you are about to over eat or eat something unhealthy. It will create discipline to enable you to have the body that you really want.

Write down what you eat for three days and then write down how you feel after each meal and then twenty minutes after each meal. Do you feel light or bloated? Keeping a food diary is a great day of motivating yourself to eat better. You will think twice about snacking on junk food. Be sure to include a healthy balance of protein, carbohydrate and your five fruit and veg a day.

Health - L

Love

Love is an extremely important part of the mental health empowerment mentoring packing. What I mean here is the ability first and foremost to love you. That's right. You must love yourself, then you can attract happier states in the people that you come into contact with. This includes family and friends and people you do not even know.

The energy or chi you give off whatever you want to call it will depend on how much you truly love yourself.

Here it is extremely important to be real, as much as you can. However, if you are particularly depressed, lacking in motivation, down in the dumps or have low self-esteem you may have to 'fake it until you make it'.

As corny as this phrase sounds, it really can work wonders.

Look in front of a mirror and look yourself in your eyes. Take ten deep breaths in and out lasting for at least three seconds in and three seconds out. So, that's one minute at least looking at you. Then, start saying I love you. Keep looking into your eyes and keep saying I love you. The first time I did this I cried with the release of emotion. I felt so grateful for being me. What surprised me was that I was actually well and in a good mood at the time when I did this and it still had a profound impact on me. Take a break for a minute and feel gratitude for everything that is good in your life, whether it's your health, the fact that you have food on the table, you are blessed with having a loving family, enjoying your work. Whatever it is, really appreciate what you have.

Then go back in front of the mirror and say "I love myself" ten to a hundred times. You will find that this too has a profound impact on your mood. This is an amazing technique that you can just say to yourself when you are on your own. The more you say it, the bigger an impact it has. I also think it to myself over and over again. This too can also have a profound impact. I think it to myself sometimes when I am swimming and I even say it whilst breathing out under water. Personal impact has a profound impact if you can do it while exercising.

All the above are amazing techniques to teach you to be kind to yourself and love yourself. They are part of the cathartic journey of being your own Mental Health Mentor so you can be interdependent and live the life of your dreams now. They enable you to take full responsibility for your life and design the life that you want to.

Loving oneself more can be a real breakthrough for people with mental health conditions. I have been working with people with mental health experiences since 2000 and have noticed that once people feel good about themselves then their mental illness disappears and happiness comes more into their lives. Remember nobody is happy all the time and nobody loves himself or herself all the time. You can remind yourself to love yourself whenever you want. You can train your mind to stop those unhappy feelings taking over. Allow yourself to love yourself and be happy and tell yourself that this is what you deserve.

Health - T

Truth

'Know thyself' is an old adage that dates back to the Ancient Greek Empire, and is still highly relevant today. The more you know yourself the more truthful you are about you own life and where you are. By being honest with yourself you can finally take full responsibility for where you are in your life. The one thing that people with mental illness suffer from more than anything is that they fail to take responsibility for where they are with their life. They are incongruent, and they blame other people for where they are and what life situation they are in. I know this as I used to do it myself constantly. Until I was 25 years old I never really took responsibility for my own life. The moment I finished writing my first draft of my autobiography on living with bipolar disorder 'A Can of Madness' I accepted that the reality was that I was 100% responsible for where my life had ended up at that moment. That made me realize that I too was therefore responsible for getting myself out of that situation. The moment that I realized that I gained so much momentum that my life was never the same again. I was torpedoed into a more positive and more fulfilling life. I began to set my own sail and whatever life threw at me I had a better way of dealing with it.

Every day I remind myself of this fact that I am responsible for where I am now and where I will be in the future. By being honest with myself I know that I can determine my own destiny and design the life of my future and therefore choose to do what I want to do on a daily basis. Sometime of course I have to be disciplined and put in the work today to reap the benefits tomorrow but that is something that al successful people do.

Recently I spent a whole day with 16 times World Darts Champion Phil Taylor. He was at the very top of my list of people I wanted to meet so somehow I managed to work out how to get to meet him... When I asked him how he had been so successful over such a long period of time he looked me smack in the eye with great intensity and said:

> *I've got one word for you Jason, dedication. Dedication is what makes me the best. Dedication for 30 years, every day. ...has made me the best player. I'm more dedicated than the rest of them. That's the secret.*

It reminded me of one of my favourite programs I used to watch when I was younger – Record Breakers. The presenter Roy Castle used to sing the song:

"Dedication is what you need if you want to be a record breaker."

Truth as I see it is the ability to be honest with yourself. Then and only then can you acquire the platform, skill and dedication needed to be your own successful mental health mentor, to live life on your terms and make your mental illness a thing of the past, to choose life and shine through it instead of suffering. Choose life, be truthful to yourself, and love yourself. Get some momentum and then you can dedicate the rest of your life to being well doing the things you want to do and having the emotion to enjoy life.

Health - H

H Hypnosis (self-hypnosis – where you focus is where you end up)

Self-Hypnosis is a massive tool in being your own number one Mental Health Mentor. The world is full of negative imagery in the media, television, newspapers, advertising and the way many people are that you come across on a daily basis. Choose to be different than the negative hypnotic culture of negativity that acts like zombies drifting across the planet. Instead tap into that amazing energy of life, the universe, God, quantum energy, frissons, chi, manifestations, attraction, etc., and use self-hypnosis as an amazing tool to catapult yourself into mental health mentoring superstar status and be a yes person who is full of life and abundance.

Yes, yes, yes. Be happy. I am happy, I am making the world a better place. I love myself, I like myself, I love the world, I am someone and I can do it. When the going gets tough – I get stronger, I make life easier, I become more fulfilled and I become more successful. I am happier, I am giving out love and I am grateful.

Self-hypnosis is a masterful tool in living a happier and more amazing life, period. It's something that you can do at any moment.

I spend time listening to personal development audio whenever I am driving in the car. I watch you tube and continually search for the words success and motivation. I do this at the start of the day so I can get the most out of the day. This makes me more decisive and forces me to be more proactive, take more action, be more positive and get more done each day than I would do otherwise.

Another really powerful form of self-hypnosis is listening to things like Paul McKenna CD's – "Instant Confidence" and "I Can Make you Happy" are two of the best. The beauty here is that you can just lie down and listen to them without distraction and you do not have to think you just relax and let your subconscious mind take over. They are so powerful that I have been recommending them to clients for years.

When I am a hard turbo session in my garage for my Ironman training I put on Jim Rohn – "The Power of Ambition" a 6 hour free audio on you tube to pump me up. No matter how hard the turbo session is and believe me some of them are excruciatingly hard they seem easier. If I have a really hard session, I will put

Tony Robbins on and that gives me so much momentum that I blast the session like a man possessed or dare I say it like a professional athlete. Gotta dream right, lol...

Coaching

C Congruency (everything in your life needs to be congruent)
O Organised
A Action
C Coach yourself
H Highlight
I Inspiration
N Nurturing (every single day)
G Goal Setting daily it's a must

Coaching - C

Congruency

Proficient congruency is an absolute must if you want to be a master at mental health mentoring yourself to happiness. You'd be amazed at people in all walks of life who may appear to be successful, happy or have it all but are incongruent in some way, shape or form.

Whether it's the multi-millionaire sales person who appears to be an inspiration and happy family but deep down they know they are not serving their clients and they are actually damaging them.

Just look at Lance Armstrong, for many years believed to have been probably the greatest athlete of all time and cancer survivor raising millions for charity and then the whole world discovers he cheated. Look at Tiger Woods the greatest golfer in the world for well over a decade and then stories come out about his infidelity.

Celebrities seeming to have it all and then they end up in the Priory.

So many people's life are out of balance, they have one thing but they lack something else. The ultimate mental health mentoring is about consistency in every aspect of one's life. Of course there are times when parts of one's life goes better than other aspects and this is where goal setting, honest and self-evaluation really help.

Break down your life into different sections: happiness, finances, family, love, fitness, health, spirituality, contribution, fulfilment, etc. Then measure yourself in each area. Write down your three most important goals in each area for yourself for the next twelve months.

In order to get real congruency in your life I advise you to do goal setting every day. The best place to do this nowadays is on your mobile phone. I set my goals in the notes section of my phone. It's easily backed up and I can amend it whenever I want as I carry my phone round with me most of the time.

I write my daily goals in the first person and in the present tense on my calendar section. I also break down my day into different times, so I can fit my training in, spend time with my children and partner, fit my work commitments in, and spend time writing or doing whatever else I have decided to do in advance. This makes me much more organized and enable me to get much more done in a day that I would do otherwise.

Coaching -- O

Organised

Get organized. If you want to mentor yourself to good mental health then organize your life. Be a doer but map your life out as well. The best way to organize yourself these days is probably on your mobile phone in the notes section and/or by using your calendar. I use an iPhone and organize my life into several categories. I have one for my Ironman training. Every day I write down the date, training I did and how it went. Then I have a financial section which has a list of all my savings, goals and any issues, etc. I also have a business notes section with priorities, actions and brainstorming – I add and delete as appropriate, delegate or discuss in meetings, etc. Then I also have a Happiness section – here I list things that make me happy, that I am grateful for, etc. I look at this rarely but when I do it really does put my life back into perspective and give me the happiness boost I need the time that I look at it and it can give me great momentum, I also have a planning section where I have set all kinds of goals until the year 3000. One has to be optimistic right.

I also have a family/growth section where I put things that make my partner happy, the kids swimming lessons in and the size of their feet and the date, etc., or their school results.

I also have a to-do list that I add to and delete as appropriate. By having all these different sections on my phone I am able to maintain a pretty consistent balance of every aspect of my life. Of course at certain times some parts of my life are more fulfilled than others, but so is everyone's.

Think about how your life is structured into different sections and break it down. For example.

1) Work/Business
2) Finances
3) Exercise
4) Family
5) Relationships
6) Happiness
7) Goals
8) To do list

The way I see it the more organized you are the better. The more you break your life down into segments the more you can see where you are doing well and where you are lacking in one area.

Also think about things that you think are keeping you organized but are actually distracting you. For example, the most successful people generally look at their emails only twice a day. The most likely times are 11.00 and 3.00pm. This way you can be more pro-active on actually getting things done instead of being reactive.

Coaching - A

Action

Of course it's great being organized but what you need to do is make sure you take action. What you want to avoid doing is organizing too much and end up being a procrastinator. That really would be wasting your energy and talent. Many people misunderstand action. In order to be successful you just need to start something and then the motivation comes from that. Many people just sit watching their dreams disappearing looking for motivation that is never going to arrive. Motivation does not just come up to you and give you a helping hand, you need to take action in order to get results.

Most super successful people start taking action on something even before they believe it is possible. By taking action the impossible suddenly becomes possible.

Coaching - C

Coach Yourself

Mentoring yourself is critical to living an abundant, fulfilled and happy life. We all have the ability to make ourselves happy or unhappy by the story we constantly put in our own heads. Our thought determine our actions and our actions determines where we end up in live. Where we focus is where we end up. We have to tell ourselves in all of our senses to be positive and live life to the fullest. We have to remove any negative thoughts in our head and turn them around and make them positive, Turn negative images into positive ones, turn negative feelings into positive ones, etc. There are thousands of different kinds of self-help tools that have been developed over the years that are all useful and many claim to be the only way of doing something or the best way of leading a happier life or living the life of one's dreams.

Let's take a reality check. It all comes down to common sense. People with mental illness and who are trapped in negative mental health experiences need to snap out of it by re programming their brain, thoughts, visions, hearing into more positive things. Then by taking action on something the motivation will follow.

Mentoring yourself is the guide to true happiness. Then you do not have to be reliant on any new magical system that is being marketed on the internet. There are two billion people online as I write this in 2014. By 2020 there will be six billion people on the internet. Choose now to mentor yourself and take responsibility for your own situation and happiness and become the leader of your own life. Then you will be the master of your own destiny and ultimately in control of your own mental health and turn that mental health into happiness.

Coaching - H

Highlight

Highlight. Highlight yourself to a better life. What do I mean? Well congratulate yourself for the things that you do well and use positive triggers and reinforce them. So many people lead their lives day to day on achievement and getting things done and forget to congratulate what they are achieving and already achieving. Highlighting these moments are part of enjoying life's journey. Remember that happiness is a journey and not a destination. If you always look for happiness you will never find it. It comes from within. This sounds so simple but it is yet so profound.

Also tell the people you love and like how much you appreciate them and see the impact that this not only has on their lives and their state, but feel the positive feelings that this brings to your life, too.

Highlighting your successes will give you more happiness. People who focus on their mental health experiences need to give themselves more love at every moment and every day and then they will lead happier lives.

Coaching - I

Inspiration

Inspiration comes from so many sources that it is contagious. You can search inspiration on you tube and find some amazing video compilations of motivational speakers, successful business people and sports stars. Inspiration comes from finding mentors in your own life. The great thing here is that they can be people that you do not even know personally. You can gain inspiration from the most successful people in the history of the world. Fill your mind with mental magic as opposed to mental trash. We are bombarded by negative news online and on the television. Arrange your life so that what you hear, see and feel is 100 times more positive than negative and not the other way round and you will start to see a transformation in how you think, act and. Live and feel on a daily and momentary basis.

You will then have turned your life around. By filling your mind, eyes and heart with mental magic you will feel better every second and more positive things will come into your life. You will then take action on those little things that before you told yourself you could not do as you did not have the confidence or potential or take action on those things that you were going to put off until tomorrow.

Inspire yourself and inspire others around you. Then you are a force for good in the world and in your community. Then your 'mental illness mindset' can be a thing of the past.

Coaching - N

Nurturing (every single day)

Nurturing yourself is so, so, so important. Be kind to yourself. Make sure you are hydrated. Drink enough water. This alone will make your brain more active and make you more active. You will be amazed how many people are dehydrated on a daily basis. Eat healthily. You can still eat healthily even if you do not have much money. You can buy chicken, potatoes and carrots from a supermarket, for example. This has all the protein, nutrients and carbohydrates you need for a healthy meal.

Make sure that you get enough sleep. Every person that I have ever come across with mental health experiences has had problems sleeping at one time another or does not give themselves enough sleep. For people with Bipolar Disorder for example, lack of sleep is what ends up causing the mania, time and time again.

You must be kind to yourself. Rest when you need to, eat and drink healthily. Give yourself kind thoughts. Spend time with people who are good to you and make your life better in some way as much as possible. Do not let other people drag you down. If they are then you really need to decide whether you want them in your life or give them an ultimatum to change. Feel good about yourself and you will attract happier people. Cannot find them outside your house – find them in a book, on you tube. Dedicate at least an hour a day to forcing yourself to watch or experience positive information. Stop watching the news for ten days and see how you feel. Less anxious and more positive. I guarantee it!

Coaching - G

Goal Setting

Everything we have discussed in this book has been aimed to get you to lead a happier more fulfilled life and break down that mental health bug once and for all. Goal setting is an absolute must in the sense that by setting goal so every day you will immediately have the opportunity to put yourself in the happier percentage of society.

There have been lots of studies on this in the personal development industry over the years. Some of them are even believed to have been made up however. Brian Tracy one of the personal development greats is reported to have said "Even if the studies were not true then they should be". I agree.

Do you think Michael Jordan became the best basketball player of all time by not setting goals? Of course not. He worked every day on his craft to become the best. Recently, I interviewed Mirinda Carfrae – three time Ironman World Champion – she said that she became the best by finding everything out about the sport and then putting the effort in. I also interviewed Frederick Van Lierde recently – Ironman World Champion 2013. I asked him how he became successful. He said: "working hard and setting goals".

There is no magic button you can press to snap out of your mental illness and create mental magic except to set goals and to work hard on them every single day of your life. Sure, we all have set backs but it's how you react to them that makes the difference to how your life turns out not what happens to you.

Make your life better by giving yourself better thoughts every moment.

Write your goals down every day on your mobile phone. Spend five to fifteen minutes a day writing them down. Write ten a day in the first person, in the present tense and if you have already achieved them. Make them specific as well.

Write your dreams down as if you have already achieved them and then get on with doing them baby step by step at first.

Most people massively over estimate what they can do in one year but underestimate what they can do in ten, twenty, thirty, forty years' time.

I remember wanting to do an Ironman. I was thirty-seven years of age, had not swam a mile since I was nine years old, had never ran more than five kilometres and have never cycled more than ten miles at a time. By using all the techniques I have shared with you in this book I was able to become an Ironman athlete within eleven months of first thinking about doing it.

For those of you who do not know. The ironman consists of a 2.4 mile swim with 3000 people swimming next to each other, a 112 mile bike ride – and it was 35 degrees in the heat, followed by running a full 26.2 mile marathon all in a row.

Finishing the Ironman was a great experience and that is all I want for you from this book. I want you to have a great experience reading the book and I want it to have an even greater impact on your life.

Please – give yourself mental magic. Become your own Mental Health Mentor. Take responsibility for where you are in your life and dream big about where you want to be. Study happiness, enjoy life along the way and I hope that happiness lives inside of you and the mental health experiences catapult into another Galaxy and disintegrate forever.

Stay well and be happy,

Jason Pegler

www.ingramcontent.com/pod-product-compliance
Lightning Source LLC
Chambersburg PA
CBHW031142270326
41931CB00007B/657